WHat will You WeAR To go SWIMMing?

To Philip

WHat will You weAR To go SwIMMing?

AND OTHER NEW POEMS FOR THE SCHOOL YEAR

Lois Rock

LION
Children's Books

Text by Lois Rock
This edition copyright © 2002 Lion Publishing

The moral rights of the author
have been asserted

Published by
Lion Publishing plc
Mayfield House, 256 Banbury Road,
Oxford OX2 7DH, England
www.lion-publishing.co.uk
ISBN 0 7459 4574 0

First edition 2002
1 3 5 7 9 10 8 6 4 2 0

A catalogue record for this book is available
from the British Library

Typeset in 12/16.5 Latin 725 BT
Printed and bound in Great Britain by
Cox & Wyman, Reading

Contents

Spring term

Summer term

Autumn term

1 Autumn

Autumn sometimes feels like an ending… but when one thing ends, something new begins.

The last of summer

The last of summer
with its wide blue sky
where the white clouds float
and the songbirds fly.

The first of autumn
with its rust and grey
where the gold and green
slowly fade away.

As the cold grey rain
fills the pale pearl sky:
time to come indoors
to the warm and dry.

A tree for tomorrow

I will plant a tree for tomorrow
in honour of yesterday
when the sun warmed the leaves
and the flowers and the seeds
and the breeze threw them all away.

Chilly autumn

Autumn has given the poor bare earth
a million leaves of gold.
Now it has only an old fir tree
to keep itself warm in the cold.

Autumn is the season

Autumn is the season when the summer leaves die
Autumn is the season when the wild geese fly
Autumn is the season when the west winds sigh
Autumn is the season when we say goodbye.

Autumn treasure

Autumn is a rich tycoon
counting in the treasure
from earth and seed invested
in every kind of weather.
Profits have grown steadily
in all the sun and rain
yielding berries, fruits and nuts
and bags of golden grain.

2 Harvest

Only a few people in this country harvest their own crops these days… but if you have ever tried to grow anything, you will understand how hard they have to work.

The vegetable plot

Remember, remember in dreary September
The fate of the vegetable plot:
Where, all through the season,
For some puzzling reason,
Though weeds have grown, your seeds have not.

The hopeful gardener

Sow the seeds with hopefulness
and lay them in a row.
Cover them and label them
for they will surely grow.

Watch the row with hopefulness
but wait at least a day.
Actually, the seeds won't grow
until you go away.

Leave the row forgetfully
and moan about the rain.
Go and play on sunny days –
it's time to look again.

All the tall plants that you see
most probably are weeds.
Those part-eaten spindly things
are what's grown from your seeds.

Hoe most conscientiously
and lift weeds by the root.
Make space for your little plants
so they can really shoot.

They'll grow to maturity
if you get the weather.
Then you'll have to harvest them
– all of them together:

radishes in millions
and green beans by the score;
half a ton of lettuces
you don't want any more.

Jet-set veg

Every day is harvest-time
At the superstore
Apples from America
Beets from Bangalore
Cabbage from the Caucasus
Raced to us by air
What's the price, I wonder, of
A vegetable's fare?

A gardener's wisdom

A garden, says my gran – and she should know –
is not so much about what you grow
and the brightly packaged seeds you sow
as knowing the shadows and the sun
and when the springtime has begun
and where and why the busy ants run
through the brown and crumbly soil
and all the days of patient toil
it takes to lift the weeds that spoil
the carefully raked and tended plot
intended for vegetables and not
for wild things; and to take the rotting
leaves of last year to the heap
where they can crumble into deep
brown compost to feed the sleeping
earth: our patient home, the place
that gave us birth.

Gardeners who are old

It seems that gardeners who are old
Are best at making the flowers unfold.

3 When I grow up

What do you dream of becoming? There are so many possibilities or… are you too late already? Or do you need to set your sights on something simpler?

Not today

When I grow up, I shall be star.
I might sing, or dance, or play.
But that will be when I'm old enough:
I'll just mess about today.

When I'm grown, I'll be widely known
for what I do on TV.
But I haven't been discovered yet –
today I can just be me.

When I grow up, I will also have
a private life of my own.
I'm going to practise more for that
today, by just staying home.

Too late

I dreamed of being a child celeb,
but it seems I'm already too old.
For I should have started the day I was born.
Oh, why wasn't my mother told?

I dream of a place on the list of the richest
teenagers on the earth.
But I should have made my first million pounds
a few weeks after my birth.

I'm working on being the most amazing
pensioner under the sun,
and won't believe those who say that I should
have started before I was one.

Bird's prayer

Build me a nest in the fork of a tree
With just enough room for my family and me.
Let me be safe while I look to the sky
And then, when I'm older, I'll go out and fly.

Dream

I can dream
of a place
of my own
in the sun
where I do
just what I
want to do.

I believe
that each day
is a step
on the way
to make sure
that my dream
will come true.

Wish

Peace in the day:

Peace in my school
Peace in my home
Peace in the world.

Peace in the night:

Peace in the world
Peace in my home
Peace in my heart.

4 Classroom survival

Sometimes when things are tough, a day seems like for ever.

Caught

What do you say
when you've been caught
doing the things that no one ought?

Where do you look
when you've been had
doing the things you know are bad?

How do you act
when you get home
knowing the school is going to phone?

Where can you find
a place to hide
as the guilt grows from deep inside?

Why does the sadness
feel like pain?
When will you start to live again?

Where to sit

I asked not to be in THEIR group
I wouldn't sit next to HER
I ended up in the corner
With someone who's really URGH.

I'd much rather be in YOUR group
I don't mind sitting with HIM
But please, not back in the corner
It's really and truly grim.

Choosing teams

Please please choose me for your team
because I'm really nice
and I'm certified quite free
of warts and germs and lice.

OK OK I'm not the hugest
asset to the team
but I am really really nice
and very very clean.

Test survivor

The test begins, and I'm all alone
As if by a wide, grey sea
And no one is there to help to decide
Just what to write but me.
I feel a bit like a castaway
Left on some deserted shore
And I don't know quite where to begin
Though we've done these tests before.
Perhaps I should take off my shirt and socks
And tie them to a pole
To make a flag that I could wave
With the message, please, save my soul.

The genius in the class

We've got a genius in the class:
I heard our teacher say
she's got a gifted pupil here,
she said it just today.

It could be HER for number work
or HIM for reading well
or even YOU KNOW WHO for
all the hard words she can spell.

It could be THEM – they work too hard
but, oh, they get gold stars.
You don't think it would be...? Maybe?
You're right: that's going too far?

It could be YOU, it might be ME.
Ooh, that would be quite fun...
Hey! All of us are brilliant!
It might be EVERYONE!

5 Learning to write

You can spend a lifetime learning to write.

Alphabet

Nothing is as easy as ABC –
not even XYZ,
and QRS is curiously hard
to get into my head.

Handwriting

Handwriting sometimes likes to be neat
(all on the line, like marching feet)
But sometimes it likes to mess around
(tripping and tumbling like a clown)
Sometimes it likes to drift and dream
(like a slow meandering stream)
Sometimes it wants to dip and to fly
(summertime swallows up in the sky)

Punctuation

I don't like punctuation
full stop.

A blank piece of paper

Paper is not blank;
it is an open space of
possibility.

My best eraser

My best eraser is elephant-shaped
Another is just like a flower
I've loads of erasers with great designs
But none has erasing power.

6 The power of words

You can use words to name things, and that gives them shape... words give shape even to invisible things.

The written word

Talking is words in a muddle,
all um, er, like, really, well, hey!
But writing is words that are chosen
to say just what you want to say.

Free verse

Locked in rhythm,
locked in rhyme:
a poem is sentenced to
doing time;

while, outside the iron rules of scansion, style
    and syntax
there is verse that wanders freely
in search of dreams.

Why write a poem?

Why write a poem when you can take a photo?
Focus.
Just press a button and light is locked on film.
Click.
The picture will bring memories before your eyes.
Flash.
But a poem captures the feeling of your heart.
Underline.

Hopeless with words?

I'm spending a day as a poet
I'm spending a day writing verse
I'm spending a day counting syllables
I can't think of anything worse.

I'm spending a day writing stories
But I think I've just lost the plot
It's meant to be some great enrichment day
But I rather think it is not.

I'm spending a day doing drama
We act and we dance and we sing
I thought I was hopeless at literature
But I've found – the play is the thing!

Words for ever

Imagine a world with no paper,
no pencils, no pens and no ink,
no blackboards, no chalk,
no computers, in short, just
no way to record what you think.

Imagine you'd dreamed up a poem
so lovely you knew that you must
recall it for ever.
Just what would you do?
You'd write, with your finger, in dust.

7 Searching for peace

How is it that so many people in the world want peace, and yet the wars go on? That is one of the great puzzles that poems can explore… and maybe some poems will help bring peace.

The wall between us

Between us is a wall of war,
Wall of concrete, wall of wire,
Wall of deeply rooted hatred,
Wall of angry bullet fire.

On the wall I write a poem:
Words of hope and words of peace;
On your side, you paint a picture
Of the time when war will cease.

On that day, we'll bring you flowers;
You'll bring fruit grown in your land.
We will celebrate together –
Sisters, brothers, hand in hand.

Peace tomorrow

I shall make peace, yes,
for I believe in peace.
I shall make peace tomorrow morning,
at the first call of the dove.

But not tonight:
for tonight I shall sit and brood
while the sun sets blood red
in a violent crimson sky,

and the shadows of the night
take the world down,
down into the pit
of dark and troubled dreams.

But wait: perhaps I shall take
one last ray of golden light
from the setting sun
to light my way till dawn.

The olive tree

The olive tree I thought was dead
has opened new green leaves instead
and where the landmines tore the earth
now poppies dance with joy and mirth.

The doves build nests, they coo and sigh
beside the fields where corn grows high
and grapes hang heavy on the vine,
and those who fought share bread and wine.

We must make war

'We must make war,' said the government.
'We know that this war is just.'
What can be fair about bombing homes
and turning them all to dust?

'We can make war,' said the government,
'without shedding too much blood.'
So why are there bodies, cold and grey,
lying face down in the mud?

'We won the war,' said the government,
'and now we'll enforce the peace.'
So why do they keep their guns in place?
Why are no prisoners released?

'We must make war,' said the government,
'to bring all wars to an end.'
But how can a war stop the fighting?
How can a war make us friends?

Inner peace

How can the angry world ever find peace?
When will the gentle years start?
I have no answer, so I shall begin
to let peace grow in my heart.

8 Lunch

Lunch is not a life-and-death drama. Is it? Oh, perhaps it is.

Will you last till lunch?

I surely won't live until lunch-time
I feel myself growing old
And if, by some chance, I should make it
My lunch will be covered in mould.

My lunch

Marcia has a gourmet lunch,
packed by Marcia's mum;
Kelly's lunch is healthy,
so Kelly's looking glum.
Ben just scooped a bag of things
found on the larder shelf;
and mine is just predictable:
I packed it all myself.

Salad for dinner

Why do we have to have salad for dinner
Just 'cos the canteen staff wish they were thinner?
They're all obsessed with the size of their hips
And as a result we don't ever get chips.

The unwashed lunchbox

I didn't wash my lunchbox
the day we finished term.
And now, just two weeks later,
I find it's full of germs.

The germs are green and hairy
and some have brownish dots.
Mum might want to wash the box
but I would rather not.

She could wash the green away
but would the germs be dead?
Would they lurk invisibly
and bump me off instead?

When I get my new lunchbox
I'll wash it every day
with soap and disinfectant
to keep the germs away.

The best lunch of all

If I bring lunch with me from home
I end up sitting with Trish;
she eats that dodgy salad stuff
with pasta and tuna fish.

If I have dinner in the hall
I end up sitting with Joe;
he always spatters the ketchup
further than ketchup should go.

If I buy lunch from the tuck shop
I end up sitting with you;
we both love crisps and chocolate
so that is what we will do.

9 A little bit spooky

Do you get scared by spooky stuff? Why not look at it coolly and see if it turns out to be nothing at all…

I'm not afraid

I'm not afraid of spiders
and I'm not afraid of snails,
I'm not afraid of night-time cats
that mewl and screech and wail.

I'm not afraid of shadows
and I'm not afraid of night,
I'm not afraid to be alone
beneath the moon's pale light.

I'm not afraid of spooky tales,
I don't believe in ghosts.
I'm not sure I can say if there's
one thing that scares me most.

I'm bothered by the sense of doom
you sometimes get in dreams,
but most things supernatural
are really just a scream.

The ghost in the back of the house

I think there's a ghost in the back of our house
who likes to run up the stairs:
a cowardly ghost who only comes out
when nobody else is there.
I can't say that I've ever seen him –
he doesn't touch anyone's stuff –
but I wish the wind would just blow him away
in one supernatural puff.

The enchanted prince

A girl frog sat on a lily pad
Wiping away a tear:
'I wish, oh, I wish for a bullfrog
To some day find me here.'

A handsome prince came riding along.
'Oh, kiss me, Frog,' he cried,
'For I am held by a wicked spell –
I'm a bullfrog deep inside.'

'Hop off,' she croaked, 'and leave me alone.'
And then, as you might guess,
The poor old enchanted bullfrog left
And married a princess.

Treat or trick

We bought tickets for the haunted house ride,
me and my friend,
and the ticket man tried to scare us.

He put on a spooky voice and said,
'Strange things happen in this world
that the wise cannot explain.'

'True,' I replied.
'I can't explain why you've charged us the
    adult price when we're only kids.'

That made him jump.

The day that the aliens came to school

The day that the aliens came to school
was a day when we all had fun.
We put loads of green slime in the pool
which then turned pink in the sun.

They put a force field round the pitch
where normally we play ball
and we threw hoops and balls and sticks
but nothing went in at all.

We let them play with the computers
and they logged us into Mars
and all of the work that we printed
came covered in golden stars.

We waved as their spaceship flew away.
It felt a bit sad and strange,
but soon it's our turn to go visit them
as part of an alien exchange.

10 Myself, yourself

What are you like? Do you like what you are like? It's worth thinking about, like it or not.

Believe in yourself

Believe in yourself and think well of others;
Believe in others and show them your love;
Believe in the greatness beyond all knowing:
Within and beyond, below and above.

Everything I do

May everything I do be a sacrament to gentleness
A step to the horizon land of white and gold
A seed that I sow in the earth of everlastingness
Reaching up to heaven as its leaves unfold.

The world of me

My indoor world
is a tumbledown house
of trash and treasure
all mixed together.

My outdoor world
is an overgrown patch
so oddly adorned
with flower and thorn.

But in my dreams
all shimmering bright
is a sunshine garden
of love and pardon.

How to hide

I'm not at all sure that I dare to be me
I think that the outlook is bleak
I think that it's safer to try to pretend
That I am just one of the clique.

Take a look inside your soul

Take a look inside your soul:
list the things you see.
Do you like the person
you are turning out to be?

Take a look inside your soul:
anything to change –
anything you'd like to
tidy up or rearrange?

Take a look inside your soul:
very average stuff.
Just the sort that always needs
forgiveness, hope and love.

11 Home Life

Have you noticed that home life and school life don't always seem to fit?

The right stuff

I'm never forgiving my mother
I'm never forgiving my dad
They bought me the wrong sort of school bag
They are so incredibly sad.

I know that they're not made of money
But why can't they just show some taste
I won't use the thing they just bought me
So all of it's going to waste.

I'm going to get a bin liner
I'll use that for ever instead
I won't use that school bag, not ever
No, not even when I am dead.

The untidy room

Just how can I tidy my room up?
Just how can I tidy my dreams?
The things that look battered and broken
Are not just the rubbish they seem
They're fragments of 'Do-you-remember?'
They're wish-lists of 'Maybe-one-day'
They're worth more than all you can bribe me
I won't throw my treasure away.

Some dads

Some dads help with the school computers
Some dads help with sport
Some dads help with the wildlife garden…
My dad's not that sort.

My dad can't be free in the daytime
Nor at the weekend
My dad's not a great school supporter
But he's still my friend.

My mum and the bike

My mum took me to the bike shop.

'What sort of bike do you want?' she asked.
I said, 'I want a road bike.'

'Oh, you can't have a road bike,' said my mum.
'I don't want you riding on the roads.
It's too dangerous.'

'OK,' I said, 'I'll have an off-road bike.'

'Oh, you can't have an off-road bike,' said my mum.
'I don't want you riding off the roads.
It's too dangerous.'

'OK,' I said. 'I'll have a goldfish.
We can go nowhere together.'

The waiting mums

The mums are all there, waiting
Just waiting at the gate.
I fumble with my bag and stuff
I want to get there late.

I don't want Mum to worry
I love her in my thoughts
But I am so embarrassed
When she turns up in shorts.

12 Music

What sort of music do you like?

The bell

In an antique shop I found a bell.
The man said, 'Take it, for I can't sell
the thing.' What is the price of the mellow
ringing chimes that cast their own spell
of magic gold and make all things well?

The big school band

I'd like to play in the big school band,
but I can't yet play anything.
And the trouble is, I don't have the pluck
for something with lots of strings.

I'd like to play in the big school band,
but the worry is, I don't know
if I have enough of the right sort of puff
for the kinds of things that you blow.

I'd like to play in the big school band:
I would like to give it a bash.
So I'm going to thump on the old kettle drums
and make the gold cymbals crash.

A different talent

I don't want to sing in the concert
I don't want to star in the play
But if you like I'll paint scenery
Then quietly hide away.

Recorders

Emily's recorder
Is made of solid wood
Her dad bought it in Germany
And it looks really good.

My recorder's plastic
It's brown with bits of white
I think that if I practised more
It might just sound all right.

Dan got his recorder
For some pence at some car boot
But, oh, when Dan starts playing
It becomes a magic flute.

The music lover

Some people's music is dreamily soft
with cellos and old violins;
some people's music is brassily loud
with tooting and trumpeting things;
some people only make music to sell –
what drives them is greed and ambition;
and me, I can't really make music at all –
I just like to sit back and listen.

13 Christmas

What is Christmas really all about?

Christmas for free

Christmas is expensive, my grandma said to me,
Except for Christmas starlight – that shines on earth
   for free,
And frost like silver tinsel on every woodland tree
And all the love that we can share together, you
   and me.

The average Christmas

The average Christmas costs one thousand pounds –
Well, that's what the TV show said;
Let's cancel the presents from old Santa Claus
And go off to Lapland instead!

Christmas presents

I really love Christmas Eve
when we put the presents under the tree:
a gleeful heap of promises
in red and green
gold and silver
tags and ribbons
and loads and loads of love.

And then, on Christmas Day,
there are splendid things to see:
gadgets and gizmos
toys and socks
nuts and chocolates
and foaming bath perfumes in exotic bottles.
But somehow the magic has gone.

Inside I know
that what I really wanted
(although it wasn't on my list)
was for all the gift-wrapped promises to come true
for all the parcels to spill over
not with shredded tissue paper
but with joyful love and happy laughter
and to be able to reach down and find…

Christmas!

What do you want for Christmas?

'For Christmas, would you like some gold?'
I'd rather just have money.
'And what about some frankincense?'
Come on, you're being funny.

And what is more, I don't want... 'No!
I've gone and bought the myrrh!'
*You could have asked me for a list
of things that I'd prefer.*

'You're not exactly Jesus then?'
*Oh, no. I'm plain old me.
And I want fairly normal gifts
left underneath the tree:*

*I'll have this season's latest fad,
to be like all my friends
And chocolate that will last me, oh,
at least till this year ends.*

'But Christmas gifts should be much more –
they should have lasting worth.'
*May I suggest good will to all
and maybe peace on earth.*

Shop till you drop

'Shop till you drop this Christmas.'
Well, that's what everyone said.
Is that 'till you drop the parcels',
or else 'till you drop down dead'?

'Eat all you can this Christmas,
yes, eat till you're fit to burst.'
Is that 'till you burst a button',
or do they mean something worse?

'Do a good deed this Christmas.'
That's a more interesting one.
Is that 'just for self-indulgence',
or 'do good to everyone'?

SPRING term

14 Winter

Lack of sunlight in winter can sometimes get people down. But winter can be very beautiful in its own way.

Winter misery

It's horribly foggy
and horribly rainy
and horribly chilly and grey.

I don't feel bold
to face the cold –
I don't want to go out today.

The first snow

For the first time there is snow
and I simply do not know
how something quite so joyful
can fall from a frowning sky
to the sullen world below.

Does the frost-spangled wind blow
from that time so long ago
when all the world was perfect:
pure and clean and untrampled
and free from every sorrow?

Winter sunrise (haiku 5-7-5)

Dawn of frost and grey
and then the sky fire rises
red with cheerfulness.

Winter's morning

Have you seen the frostfall
Of a winter's morning
Sparkling with white magic
In the cold blue dawning?

Winter clothes

I love the puffy, fluffy things we wear against
   the cold
The snuggly, tuggly scarves and huggly hats
The steady, tready wellies and the wriggly, tiggly
   socks
and the roly poly way we all look fat.

15 Fed up with everything

If you sometimes find it hard to be all cheerful and smiley, these poems are for you. They may even be about you.

Excuses

I shouldn't have to do that job –
I did it yesterday.
It's so unfair to make me, when
the others skip away.

They always run away and hide
and leave it all to me.
I end up doing everything –
it's mean as mean can be.

At least give me a minute's break –
I'll do it in a while.

OK, OK, I'll do it now,
but don't expect a smile.

Bored

The world is dull and boring
The world is dull and grey
I feel dull and boring
Will you please go away!

Can't

They say there's no such word as can't.
I can't believe that's true.
I can't believe you can't believe
there's some things I can't do.

Overloaded

My head feels packed
With a million facts
And I'm not even twelve years old
I fear that one morning
I'll get a dire warning:
'There's no more your poor brain can hold.'

Can't, Won't, Shan't

Can't do
Won't do
Shan't do
Don't do

Shan't do
Won't do
Can't.

Won't do
Shan't do
Don't do
Can't do

Don't do
Shan't do
Won't.

16 Trying harder

Does trying harder result in doing better? Maybe. Maybe not.

Try harder, do better

If you try harder
you might do better at things.

If you try better
you might do harder things.

If you try harder better,
you might do better at harder things.

If you try better harder,
you might do harder things better.

Practice

Have a go one time
Have a go two times
Have a go three times more
Have a go four times
Have a go five times
Practice is a bore.

Have a go six times
Have a go seven and
Eight times more again
Have a go nine times
Now the last time
Got it right on ten!

The to-do list

I'm writing a list of things TO DO,
another of things TO DON'T.
And some of the things TO DON'T, I will,
and some things TO DO, I won't.

Going somewhere

Some people are best at maths.
They are with numbers
like police officers in a crowd
keeping everyone in line
and making them follow the rules
and arresting any protestors on the spot.

Some people are best at language.
They are with words
like the wind in the clouds:
sometimes making fantastical pictures

and other times blowing the sky
crystal clear.

And me. I'm best at surviving.
I know how to dare and how to run
and when to be cheeky and when to keep quiet
and how to get from anywhere to anywhere.
And you can be sure of this:
I'm going somewhere.

Late

Get your skates on,
don't be late,
don't make other
people wait,
or you'll find
your only fate
is to end up
second rate.

17 Big questions

What is the world about? What is the meaning of life?

The wide, wide world

The wide, wide world of everything
The long world of for ever
The narrow world of not enough
The brief, bleak world of never.

Breathe

The world is very good
(breathe in)
The world is bad
(breathe out)
The world is full of suffering
(breathe in, and then breathe out)

(breathe in)
The world is beautiful
(breathe out)
Yet all decays
(breathe in)
for life is here and now,
breathe on for all your days.

Pants

I sometimes think that the world is pants
It's certainly not fantastic
And most things finally let you down –
Including your knicker elastic.

Past, present, future

I have everything of the present
I have memories of the past
I have hopes and plans for the future
I am searching for what really lasts.

The wide everywhere

I don't feel afraid
to look up to the sky
and its miles and miles of blue;
for in the clear air
and the wide everywhere
is the love that surrounds me and you.

18 Bullying

No one should have to put up with bullying.

Ignored

I don't get bullied
I'm just left ignored
By those who giggle in groups
I wait on the side
But I'm not sure I hide
The way my confidence droops.

Standing up to the bullies

I dream of standing up to the bullies.
In my dream I hear the sinister crinch and crunch
  as the gang scuffle up behind me.
I hear the gurgling sniggling chortling as they fan
  out around me
like hunters spreading a net.
Then in my dream I turn and look:
suddenly their hoots and howls are silenced...
they cringe away, trying to remember a few brave
  insults
before they nudge and dip and turn and run like
  cowards
for they have seen the real me:
the real, average, OK, have-a-go, give-it-try,
  do-my-best kid that I am
and that alone scares them to bits.
And my dream is truer than their lies.

Only joking

We were only joking.
We didn't want anything to get broken.

We were only joking.
We didn't want it all to end up in tears.

We were only joking.
We didn't want to start war in the playground.

Can't we just forget it?
There are some jokes that will mock you
   through the years.

Gossip

There's a whisper lisping drifting through snigger
   giggling shadows
There's a winking hinting hissing that it's true
There's a rumour prowling growling round the
   scowling lowering corners
and the whisper is, 'There's something wrong
   with you.'

War in the playground

There's war in the playground, you have to know
where you and your friends are allowed to go.
If you cross the lines, they'll give you the look
and later on someone will trash your books.
The ringleaders all know how to pretend
to the playground staff that they're being friends.
And no one dares tell that our smiling school
is really a place where the bullies rule.

19 Everything must die

The pattern of the seasons is a constant reminder that everything must die... which can lead on to wondering what that means about life.

A quiet place to sit and think

I used to like the pond.
Well, it isn't a pond really.
It's just a rather marshy place
but in the spring the willow tree unfolds green
  leaves
and there are wild daffodils and yellow irises
and it's just a quiet place to sit and think.

I used to like the pond.
Well, it isn't a pond really.
It's just a rather tussocky place
but in the summer the willow tree is shady
and the marsh marigolds are bright and the
  dragonflies hover
and it's just a quiet place to sit and think.

I used to like the pond.
Well, it isn't a pond really.
It's just a rather soggy place
but in the autumn the willow tree is golden when
  sun is not

and bright birds twitter among the reeds
and it's just a quiet place to sit and think.

I used to like the pond.
It's really only a pond in winter
when the grey rains fill it to overflowing
and it spreads out beyond the roots of the bare
  willow tree
and drowns the reeds.

I didn't know the person they found there.
They said he went out on the ice
and when it broke he slipped underneath
and couldn't get out.

But you can't blame the earth,
for it is only doing what earth must...
holding the world in its arms through birth and death.
And you can't blame the water,
for it is only doing what water must...
freezing with the frost and melting with the sun.

So perhaps, in the spring,
I shall go back down to watch the willow coming
  into leaf
and the daffodils and irises unfolding their petals
and in that quiet place
I shall sit and think.

My funeral

I'm not going to go to my funeral.
Well, I'll be there in body, I suppose,
but not in spirit. So don't spend a lot on my body
but on things that will lift your spirits.

Do our relatives watch us?

Do our relatives watch us from heaven
As if we were some kind of zoo?
Do they float by on clouds with a spyglass
To catch all the sly things we do?
Do they care that we argue and bicker
In all of that everyday strife?
If they do, I've got something to tell them,
And here it is: go get a life.

The edge of what we can see

The horizon is not
the end of the world
but the edge of what we can see;

and death is not
the end of a life
but the edge of eternity.

There will be justice one day

There will be justice one day,
I know it.

There will be some great judgment day,
when everyone will assemble before God,
and God will look at each person in turn,
into their eyes, into their heart, into their soul,
and God will know even better than they do
what there is within them that is good
and what there is within them that is wicked.
And God will cleanse them with a pure, fierce justice
and forgive with a kind and gentle love.

There will be justice one day,
I know it.

20 Something to do with art

Arty things tend to cause a bit of chaos. From the chaos, you might create something beautiful. Sometimes things stay in chaos!

I think that I really like painting

I think that I really like painting
I like both to dip and to splash
To drip and to swirl and to spatter
With all kinds of colours that clash.

I think that I really like painting
With brushes as thin as a hair
And others so wide I can paint seas and skies
And let colour wash everywhere.

I think that I really like painting
And conjuring magical lands
With colour; it seems that impossible dreams
Come true by the skill of my hands.

Sketchbook

When you travel, just take a pencil
(it helps to travel light)
And a book of clean white paper
(you don't need lines to write)
You can jot down all your memories
(you are allowed to draw)
Of places you have been
And the amazing things you saw.

Classroom scissors

How many scissors does our classroom need
for everyone to always have a pair?
It needs twice as many as there are of us
and about another twenty-seven spare.

Here are the crafts we made

Here are the crafts we made, all in a row
I can tell mine at a glance, and I know
that, however skilfully they are arranged,
mine will stick out, 'cos it looks really strange.

Show and tell

Tomorrow morning is show and tell.
I want to hide, and I dare not tell
all about the droopy techno thing
that I had to make with card and string.
It just doesn't work; I knew it wouldn't
but then my teacher said that I shouldn't
just throw it away. What could I do?
My only hope was to spill the glue
all over the part that should have turned...
And so there's one *good* thing I have learned –
that when it's my turn to tell and show
I'm going to tell the whole class: no.

21 Things involving numbers

Things involving numbers and measuring and recording have quite a lot in common with dog training: if you're reckless and inconsistent, they can go wildly out of control; if you learn to tame them, they're obedient and fun.

Caution

Misunderstanding
and misinformation
always result in
miscalculation.

Big numbers

'Don't be afraid of big numbers,'
said the student teacher to us;
but he didn't look very confident
facing just twenty of us.

Science experiments

The trouble with science experiments,
which makes them a bit of a bore,
is that you're supposed to get the results
that everyone got before.

I wish I could find a marble that floats,
a cork that, incredibly, sinks,
or water that won't spread out and lie flat.
All rather fun, don't you think?

I guess it would be a bit tedious
if ships sank at random at sea
but research would suddenly seem worthwhile:
right now that matters to me.

The appliance of science

A little bit of light is very strong against the dark,
but dark is not as strong against the light;
and one application of this useful information
is a torch, which is handy in the night.

The mathematician

The mathematician should master addition
and not be distraught by subtraction.
Mistakes in division will lead to derision
and multiply problems with fractions.

22 Wealth

Is money the key to happiness, or does it only lead to more expensive kinds of trouble?

The simple life

I wish I were an adventurer
Sailing so far away
Through the grey and white of the ocean
Where waves and icebergs play.

I'm not that concerned about sailing
With sheets and shrouds and things
But I want to see the albatross
Floating on outstretched wings.

I want to know how it lives alone
When all the world is bare
With no place to rest and no comfort
Except the silver air.

Nothing to carry from day to day
Nothing to lose or hide
Trusting that all it needs will be found
There in the shifting tide.

Filthy rich

I don't want to be filthy rich
(I much prefer being clean)
And stinking rich does not appeal
(I'm sure you know what I mean)
I'd really hate being loaded
(The weight would be hard to bear)
Yet there is a strange attraction
In being a millionaire.

How to open a door

I always used to think that keys
could open any door,
but now I'm finding out that money
opens many more.

A rich man went travelling

A rich man went travelling
and what did he see?
People much poorer than you and me.

A rich man went travelling
and what did he find?
Everywhere people can be unkind.

A rich man went travelling
and what did he learn?
There's more to a person than what they earn.

A rich man went travelling
and what did he gain?
The wisdom to travel back home again.

Old people don't need the money

I'd like to be wealthy while I'm a kid
'Cos then I could have lots more toys
Old people don't need the money for those –
It's not something they would enjoy.

I'd like to be wealthy while I'm a teen
'Cos then I could have lots of clothes
Old people don't really care what they wear
They don't have the body, I s'pose.

I'd like to be wealthy when I start work
'Cos then I could have a good car
Old people don't want to drive really fast
They never go out very far.

I'd like to be wealthy to buy a house
'Cos then I could have a big place
Old people don't need to have loads of rooms
They're fine in their own little space.

I'd like to be wealthy when I have kids
I'd buy them whatever they'd need
Old people only buy things for themselves
They've no growing children to feed.

I'd like to be wealthy when – oh, how strange
I've never thought how time can fly!
I think that when I find myself growing old
There'll still be things I want to buy.

23 Flickering screens

In days gone by, people didn't have screens to watch.

In my day

'In my day,' says my grandma,
'we four kids had just one bedroom to share between
    us –
there was no private den or fancy furnishings then,
    you know.
We just had to learn to manage, and it didn't hurt us.'

'In my day,' says my mum,
'we three kids had just one TV to share between us –
no extra sets or video to catch the special programmes
    then, you know.
We just had to learn to manage, and it didn't hurt us.'

Now it's my day,
and we two kids have one computer to share between us.
That's for games and homework and email and all
    kinds of important stuff.
We haven't learned to manage, and as for hurting –
HURTING? –
it's ruining my life.

Watching the box

'Take time
to smell the flowers,'
they say.
'Don't hurry through
life's summer day.'
But I'm not interested
in flowers –
I'd rather watch the box
for hours.

The flickering screen

'What are you doing this evening?'
Nothing, as far as I know.
I don't have any money to spend;
there's nowhere I want to go.
I don't belong to some stupid club –
you know the sort that I mean.
I think I'll just be flopped on the couch
in front of the flickering screen.

Fantasy friends

I think I'm happier watching the soaps
than being with people I know.
You never get caught up in bickering
just watching a TV show.
My mum always tries to make me go out
and join in with all kinds of stuff
but TV shows bring me fantasy friends
and I think they're quite good enough.

The interrupted game

Aha! I've found the secret key
(this game is getting good).
I found it in the labyrinth –
I always thought I would.

Ring ring: the phone. For me. Fake voice:
'Oh hi, it's you, that's nice…
'… You want my help?'
Mum shouts, 'Fine, go!'
Oh, thanks for that advice.

Er, think, and quick,
'Oh dear, I can't, because I'm... in a fix.
Yeah, sorry, bye.' Phew, back to game
and on to level six.

24 Getting along together

Getting along with everyday people in an everyday kind of way should be easy... should be, anyway.

Good enough friends

I wish I was a letter of the alphabet.
I don't really mind which:
I just think it would be nice
to be part of a crowd of twenty-six –
all of us a bit different
but with lots in common.

We could take it in turns to be capitals
or to dress up in fancy styles.

We'd take part in different words:
sometimes just a couple of us together,
other times a huge team of something really long
    and complicated.

In some words I could have a really dramatic part
or at least one that made a real difference;
in others I'd be almost unnoticed –
I'd just hang around quietly for the fun of it.

Sometimes, of course, we might get things
   muddled up,
or get together in words that were mean and nasty
but we could always find a way to say sorry
and to start again.

I wish I was a letter of the alphabet.

The colour of racism

Racism isn't a black and white issue.
Nor is it shades of grey.

It's more olive and brown
and peach and cream
and rosy and freckled
and pale and dark.

But beyond that superficial view
is the heart of the matter:

the heart and mind and soul
of each and every one of us.

A maggotty friend

Oh, once I had a maggotty friend
so selfish and scheming and sly.
Oh, how I wish I'd gone off on my own
and not let a day go by
of falling in with their maggotty plans
to do things that I knew were wrong.
I wish I'd not lived all those maggotty days.
Oh, why did I stay friends so long?

The nice and normal people

When the gang of in-crowd girls
begin to scream and screech
all us nice and normal people
stay well out of reach.

In-crowd, out-crowd

Part 1

I could hang out with the in-crowd but
the out-crowd are more forgiving.
Shall I be fashionable and admired
or have a life that's worth living?

Part 2

Did you see that poem about the in-crowd?
Did you see who wrote it?
It is so, soooo stupid.

I mean, honestly, it's not like we've got two heads
    or anything
just because we've got taste;
and if you want to see a MEAN person –
well, we all know who deserves to be called MEAN
not to say GOSSIPY
not to say OVERWEIGHT... like fat, like really huge,
with shoes that are, I mean UUURGGGGH.
Well, I think we know who's not in with us, then.

25 Night

As a little kid you get called indoors when it goes dark. Very sensible too... but night itself is not dangerous. It is simply dark, and it can be lovely.

The night-time sky

The night-time sky
is an upturned bowl of pewter,
grey and cold,
with a ragged hole
that lets the light shine through
from realms of gold.

Night-time rain

The night-time rain is falling down
like music from the sky:
a gentle tune of shifting skies
and dream clouds floating by.

The night-time rain is falling down:
a simple melody
of softly lapping wavelets
on the deeply sleeping sea.

Twinkle, twinkle, planet Mars

Twinkle, twinkle, planet Mars
Odd to see how close you are
Floating, sort of middle high
Like a ruby in the sky.

Actually, you're not that red
More a rosy pink instead
Pink. Hmm… for the god of war?
Not quite as I thought before.

Anyway, how's life with you?
Any rivers running through?
And, our probe, did it land right?
(Wasn't watching out that night.)

One more question: have you seen
Any creatures, strange and green?
No? I thought not. Nor have I
Seen odd saucers in the sky.

Well, that's all I've got to ask
So, enjoy, go off and bask
In the sun's amazing light
I'm quite sleepy now. Goodnight!

Shadows

Night-time shadows come rolling in
And flood all the world with grey
Drowning the path that leads to home
And stealing the land away.

Moonlight shadows come dancing by
Like shimmering silver waves
They crest and fall to float us home
And whisper that we are saved.

Lamplight shadows stand guard around
A harbour of welcome light
We walk ashore and into our home
Out of the sea of the night.

Be careful in the dark

Be careful in the dark:
be careful of potholes
and kerbstones
and snails on the pavement.

Be careful in the dark:
be careful of cats
and night owls
and moths in the lamplight.

Be careful in the dark:
be careful of fear
and worry
and wild imaginings.

Be carefree in the dark:
gather starlight
and moonlight
and tattered clouds.

26 Spring

Spring: the season that everyone loves to love. The reality can be breathtaking... or rather disappointing.

Spring is the season when...

Spring is the season
when the weeds all shoot
from mud as deep as
your wellington boots.

Spring is the season
when the fruit trees flower
then lose their petals
in a passing shower.

Spring is the season
when the tulips grow
and then get buried
in a heap of snow.

The springtime invasion

Take care! Be on your guard!
You live in a wild place.

Do not be fooled by the neat rows of paving stone
   and brick
which mark the edges of your dwelling.
Look how easily the tiny seeds invade their domain
and plant eccentric gardens filled with mosses, leaves
   and flowers.

Look out for the creatures who have taken up
   residence beside you –
spiders spreading their sticky, tangled traps,
woodlice bumbling through your home to theirs,
ants establishing their colonies and empires.

And listen... listen for the wild wind
blowing in from the great eternal everywhere
with whispered messages, chuckling laughter
and whining, whooping howls of a power that pays
   no heed
to your little rules and regulations and by-laws.

Take care! Be on your guard!
And also let your spirit dance with delight –
You live in a wild place.

Leaves

Think of leaves and think of green
'Lots of those, but have you seen
Orange leaves and even red?'
Yes, of course, but some were dead.
'What of yellow? What of pink?'
Yellow, yes, but let me think...
Well, sort of pink, and purple too,
And even some of misty blue.
Stripy leaves and leaves with spots,
Streaks and splodges, flecks and dots –
All the patterns nature weaves
In the colours of the leaves.

Spring comes slowly

January: Spring unwraps a snowdrop.
February: Spring unwraps a crocus.
March: Spring unwraps a daffodil.
Oh, hurry up or we'll be here till Christmas.

April: that's more like it!

A daffodil

A daffodil needs to be yellow
A daffodil needs to be bright
A daffodil needs to be bold enough
To scare off the frost in the night.

27 Easter

At Easter, Christians remember the story of Jesus. But it's a time to celebrate other things too: springtime, flowers, chocolate!

The Easter bunny

The Easter bunny lives in an egg
Feasting on chocolate cream
His friends all say he's a basket case
Lost in a daffodil dream.

Life comes leaping

Winter death
and springtime breath;
Winter grief
and springtime leaf;
Winter sleep
but life comes leaping
from the darkest deep.

New life

Let me capture springtime
Bright with yellow flowers
Twittering with birdsong
Glittering with showers.

Let me capture summer
Blue with sea and sky
Lazy like the seabirds
Drifting in the sky.

Let me capture autumn's
Cloak of red and gold
Darned with threads of silver
As the year grows old.

Set me free from winter's
Prison bars of rain
From earth's dark decaying
Let life spring again.

Easter is about...

Good Friday is about
burdens loaded on innocent shoulders
and nails hammered into innocent hands,
a spear piercing an innocent heart
and death enshrouding an innocent life.

Easter is about
unexpected and joyful reunions
and simple meals shared with friends,
old grievances forgiven and forgotten
and angels rolling wide the way to heaven.

Easter sunrise

Friday sunset, black and red.
Weep, for Jesus Christ is dead.

Sunday sunrise, white and gold.
Christ is risen, as foretold.

SUMMER term

28 The whole school together

When lots of people get together, what happens? People get the giggles… or things go wrong.

Assembly time

We all sit still at assembly time
(Oh, please stop jigging my arm)
And think of grand and spiritual things
(What time is the fire alarm?)
We use this time to think and reflect
(I wish all of school was sports)
On things that truly matter to us
(Have I remembered my shorts?).

One big school

Each day at school assembly
we sit in squished-up rows.
Someone breathing in your ear
and someone on your toes.
Someone singing much too loud
and someone eating sweets.
Someone scuffing up their shoes
which started out so neat.
Someone scratching at the lice
that crawl around their hair.
Others gazing blankly
with a strange, unblinking stare.
I'm not sure if anyone
is listening at all.
But I still like assembly, 'cos
it makes us one big school.

A fit of the giggles

Oh dear, I can feel my socks start to giggle
and snigger and chortle and scoff;
I'm sorry, I cannot control them today –
my socks want to laugh themselves off.

The big surprise

If the sun shines on Saturday
the fête will be in the field
and that's where the big surprise about
the raffle will be revealed.

But if it rains on Saturday
the fête will be in the hall
and there's a risk that the big surprise
will not be revealed at all.

And if it snows on Saturday
the fête won't happen this year.
So where will they put the big surprise?
There's no room to keep it here.

We really need fog from now until
that moment on Saturday
when we can reveal the big surprise:
oh no, I'm not meant to say!

The Year Six trip

The Year Six trip is to Minehead
and even the Infants know
that for a whole week in early July
that is where Year Six goes.

There's one long assembly on Minehead
so everyone gets to see
the place where they'll all be camping and
the path that leads to the sea.

They write up their projects on Minehead,
which go on display in the hall,
and then do a big presentation
to entertain us all.

A visitor came to inspect Year Six:
she asked a boy, 'Where did you go?'
And his class teacher was so annoyed
when he replied, 'I don't know.'

29 Weather

Isn't it amazing how different weather can be from day to day... from pearly mists of grey to bright, clear skies.

Rainbow

I saw a pale rainbow
nearly washed away by rain
then it evaporated
as the sun came out again.

Mist

The drifting, drizzling mist of grey
Has stolen all the world away
Oh, how much silver would you pay
To buy the golden light of day?

Wind

The wind cannot blow the world away
Because it's tied down with string
It can huff, it can puff, it can howl, it can growl
But it won't get away with a thing.

When the storm-birds sing

I'm off to everlasting land
to fetch a piece of string
to wrap around the rooftops
when the storm-birds sing.

I'm off to everlasting land
to fetch a giant boat
to gather up survivors
when the flood weeds float.

I'm off to everlasting land
to fetch a pot of glue
to stick the world together
when the sky is blue.

Weather lore

'Red in the morning, shepherds' warning.'
Oh, bad news for those who have sheep.
But what kind of weather will we get?
A blizzard? A thunderstorm? Sleet?

'Rain at seven, fine by eleven...'
But what about twenty to nine?
For goodness' sake: when I walk to school
Will I need that raincoat of mine?

'Red sky at night, shepherds' delight,'
Why? Can they knock off for their tea?
I don't care what shepherds get up to,
Just say what the weather will be!

30 Looking presentable for school

In theory, it's easy to look presentable for school, because it's pretty much the same from day to day. But there are lots of little glitches...

Get ready for today

Squiffy hair day
scuffy shoes day
grubby shirt day
photograph day.

Not my socks

The socks I've got aren't mine: they're Jane's
'cos she said hers were snatched by James
who couldn't find his after games
the day he called the girls rude names
but Jane's and mine were just the same
and he took mine, I know, I came
and saw him take them. So did Jane,
but hers were lost: that's why she blamed
the beastly James, so she reclaimed
my socks from off the feet of James
then he found his – where? In the same
place that he left them; so in shame
I walked home sockless after games
and next day Mum came and she claims
that she found mine and put my name
in them; but I know all the same
the socks I've got aren't mine: they're Jane's.

School uniform

Uniform sweatshirts
uniform grey
uniform schoolwork
uniform day.

The terrible lice

Headlice only creep and crawl
and yet, somehow, they reach us all.
We must all show dedication
to achieve eradication.

Shoe day

Tomorrow morning is shoe day
We're meant to make our shoes smart
We've got to get rid of the dirt
And the things we spilt in art.

Tomorrow morning is shoe day
We're not allowed shoes that smell
And teacher said it's much better
If we wear clean socks as well.

Tomorrow morning is shoe day
We'll all stand up in a line
I think the passing satellites
In space will pick up the shine.

31 A little bit risky

Life is a little bit risky. But how much risk is the right amount of risk?

Facing your fears

Can you face your deepest fears?
Blink away your coward tears?
Dive so deep, or climb so high?
Jump from way up in the sky?
Crawl through dark and dripping caves?
Are you really truly brave?
Are you? Have you ever dared
to admit when you are scared?

Health warnings

They've put a ban on running
for statistics show you'll fall
from time to time, but to be safe
just don't stand up at all.

They're warning about eating, too,
for scientists don't know
the true effect on human health
of anything we grow.

It's recommended not to drink
for no one can be sure
the water that's available
is absolutely pure.

And cut back on your breathing
for there's been a recent scare
about the unseen particles
all floating in the air.

Above all, give up living –
you'll have guessed the reason why:
they've proved that everyone who lives
is surely going to die.

Fear

I am walking all alone where the trees grow so tall
I am walking all alone where the dinosaurs call
I am walking all alone where the crocodiles crawl
I am walking all alone and I'm not scared at all.

Worry

I wonder, what shape is a worry? –
So huge when it waits up ahead
It fills you with fear and with trembling
Anxiety, horror and dread.

I wonder, what shape is a worry? –
So tiny when it has passed by
No more than a wisp of a shadow
And – oh! – what a waste of a sigh.

Braver than anyone else

I live on the side of danger
I live on the edge of fear
I know that I'm braver than anyone else
when nobody else is near.

32 Goldfish

Everyone has their own favourite pet.

In praise of goldfish

Sing a song of cod fish
Of mackerel and sole
But write a hymn of praise
To a goldfish in a bowl.

I love my fish

I love my fish and my fish loves me
More than the sea lions love the sea
My fish is brave and my fish is bold
Dressed in his armour of shining gold.

Friends apart

My goldfish can breathe in the water
But I need to breathe in the air
We'd like to get closer together
Oh, life is so very unfair.

My goldfish friend

Caught in the everyday round of life
with nothing to save my soul
I've found a friend who'll be mine to the end
just swimming around in a bowl.

Warning

Dear Fish, I don't want to alarm ya
With stories of things that might harm ya
But friends on their way
Just possibly may
Bring with them their own pet piranha.

33 How time flies

Time seems to go so slowly when you're looking forward to something; but when you look back, it seems like no time at all.

I wish that I was much older

I wish that I was much older
Gran wishes she was still young
Let's add the ages
And halve the result:
Oh, now I'm as old as my mum.

I wish

I wish, oh, I wish it was time to play
I wish, oh, I wish it was Saturday
I wish, oh, I wish for a holiday
– Now don't you go wishing your life away.

I dream, oh, I dream, and I think and sigh
I dream of a castle built in the sky
I dream of the things that I'd like to buy
– While you are dreaming your life will go by.

I was born luckier than you, don't you know
I was born young, and for me time is slow
It's taking a million years just to grow
– As you grow older just watch the time go.

Growing older

I wonder how it feels to grow older
And to see how your hair has turned to grey
To notice new wrinkles and new freckles
To get a little slower every day?

I wonder how it feels to grow older
And to have fewer dreams of what will be
To spend more time thinking of the old days
When I'm old, will I still feel just like me?

I wonder what things I'll best remember
Will it be anything I do today?
What tales will I have of my adventures
When things I'm doing now are yesterday?

Like the river

Like the river,
I will dance along when I am young.
Like the river,
I will hurry when I'm grown.
Like the river,
When I'm older I will take my time
Till the tide comes to take me home.

A day with the old

I thought that a day with the old would be grey
but the day with my grandma was gold.
From the light in her eyes I could tell she was wise
with a joy that will not pass away.

34 Teachers

Nice teachers. Nagging teachers. New teachers. Nightmare teachers. You can't get through school without meeting them all!

We like our teacher

We like our teacher
who is the best,
really, really kind
and smartly dressed,
strict for the right things,
truly clever,
our teacher is
the nicest ever.

I don't understand

I don't understand
I just don't understand
why it is
that when the teacher asks
'Does everyone understand?'
and there's about six boasty people
who say, 'Yes miss' really loud
she doesn't explain again
and the rest of us
never get to understand
not ever.
I just don't understand
why it is.

Why not the teachers?

Why do we have to wear uniform
when teachers can choose what to wear?

Why do we have to remember all our stuff
if teachers are allowed to forget things?

Why do we have to hurry when we hear the
  school bell
while the teachers go on walking at their own speed?

Why do we have to do as we're told
while the teachers do all of the telling?

Mad Mrs Mac

Episode 1

Our teacher is having a baby
She's off on maternity leave
And we've got this mad Mrs Mac thing
Whose voice you just wouldn't believe.

She doesn't know how to feed goldfish
She doesn't know which books we've read
I think they should have arranged things so
The goldfish could teach us instead.
…

Episode 2

Our teacher has had her new baby
It's whispered she might not come back
She might stay at home with her darling
And we'll still have mad Mrs Mac.
…

Episode 3

Our teacher will be back tomorrow
And all of us feel rather sad
'Cos that Mrs Mac is so lovely –
The best supply teacher we've had!

The departing teacher

(To the tune of 'My bonnie')

Our teacher is giving up teaching
Our teacher is giving up school
She's not going to come back, not ever,
She's not going to come back at all.

Bring back, bring back
Oh, bring back our teacher to us, to us
Bring back, bring back
Oh, bring back our teacher to us.

She's doing a round-the-world-yacht-race
She's trekking in furthest Nepal
She's diving the tropical oceans
She's not going to come back to school.

Take us, take us
Oh, please take us travelling with you, with you
Take us, take us
It sounds like a fun thing to do.

35 Change

Every year brings changes: some inviting, some scary.

Winds of change

Let the winds of change
blow out everything that's old
and blow in the kind of emptiness
where something new can enter.

What to do now

What shall I do now?
Whatever brings you joy.

What shall I do tomorrow?
Whatever brings you joy.

What shall I do when everything goes wrong?
Open your heart to sorrow,
and let it be washed with the rain of tears
till the warm winds of passing time blow the clouds
   away.

What shall I do then?
Whatever brings you joy.

Moving house

Goodbye school
and goodbye friends:
why do good things
have to end?

Goodbye house
and goodbye home
I don't want
to be alone.

Hello courage
let's explore
no point fretting
any more.

A family is like an amoeba

A family is like an amoeba:
it can grow,
change shape,
move,
split into two;
but always
its life goes on.

A puzzle

Change is fun when it means hello
and sad when it means goodbye.
Sometimes change makes me laugh for joy
and sometimes it makes me cry.

36 Thinking of the environment

There are so many ways we spoil the world; we need to work with our planet to keep it as our lovely home.

The summer brook

The winter brook flows quick and green
with swirling eddies in between
its tiny falls of sparkling spray
that curl and ripple on their way.

The summer brook is slow and grey
and choked with all we've thrown away:
old cans and bags and battered shoes
and things that we no longer use.

O God of Noah, send the rain
to wash the whole world clean again
then teach us to respect and care
for water, fire, earth and air.

Town lights

The sulphur glow of town lights
poisons the night-time sky
where brown bats flit and flutter
and grey owls flap and fly
where nightbirds churl and twitter
among the shadow trees
then moonlight brings its healing
upon a silver breeze.

I'm losing my interest in eating

I'm losing my interest in eating
I really don't think it's my fault
I'm bored with those prepackaged snack things
and biscuits with far too much salt.

I'd quite like to have an allotment
and watch my food grow from the soil
and find out what vegetables taste like
without any ketchup or oil.

I want to make compost from peelings
not mountains of bright plastic waste
I'm losing my interest in eating
until I find something that tastes.

The smell of school

The smell of school
of mud and shoes
of newly disinfected loos
of glue and clay
of chalk and ink
of polishes
that really stink
yet where the hedge, abandoned, grows
the wild scent of briar and rose.

Life force

The dust, it blows in from the cosmic brown
to cover the earth with grace;
to lay a soft blanket of gentle soil
on land we have turned to waste.

The rain, it blows in from the cosmic blue
to water the world with love;
to flood the polluted rivers and seas
with purity from above.

The seeds, they blow in from the cosmic green
to clothe all the world with care;
to bind down the soil, then slowly uncoil
their leaves on a world left bare.

The sun, it shines down from the cosmic gold
with power and warmth and light;
to scatter the thieves who plunder with greed
a world made for our delight.

37 Summer

The light, the sunshine, the downpours, the holidays...

Walking home

I like walking to school in autumn
when the spiders' webs on hedges and railings
    are hung with dewdrops.

I like walking to school in winter
when the low morning sun comes slanting over the
    rooftops.

I like walking to school in spring
when new green seedlings in the gutter open their
    hands to the light.

But in summer
I like walking home from school
to the long, long golden evenings and the short silver
    nights.

A house of willow

I dream of a house made of willow trees
with branches that interweave
where I could live deep in the cool green shade
among the flickering leaves.

I dream of a house by the river's bank
where kingfishers dip and dive
and wagtails fly their fluttering dance
and all the world is alive.

I dream of a house made of summertime
that cannot be bought or sold
whose spirit will fly to the autumn sky
when I and my house are old.

A long weekend in August

A long weekend in August and the sky is grey with
rain,
and with each falling raindrop summer trickles down
the drain.
We pack our beach things in the loft and make a
dreary list
of things we're meant to have for school; I really
haven't missed
the hurried getting up on time, the dashing up the
stairs,
to gather books and lunch and kit left lying
everywhere.
Is half term very far away? Will it be Christmas soon?
Not yet: it's still the middle of a rainy afternoon.

Stifling hot

It's stifling hot
and the heavy air
clings to my clothes
and drags at my hair.

It's stifling hot
even in the shade
I droop like a flower
about to fade.

It's stifling hot
and I watch the sun
melt in the sky
till the day is done.

Summer thunder

Roll the sky with thunder
split the sky with light
watch the birds fly nestwards
in a swift and startled flight.

Gently squeeze the stormclouds
so the heavy rain
washes through the grimy air
and makes it clean again.

38 Summer sports

Time for sports: time playing, time suffering, time losing, time winning.

Winners and losers

Sing praise to the winners of races
And give them a medal of gold
A sign that they trained and they practised
That they were determined and bold.

To those that come second, give silver
And bronze to those running in third
Let them stand together, all smiling
They've beaten the rest of the herd.

The people in fourth place need comfort
They did really well – but not quite
As well as they'd hoped, and they'll sniffle
A bit about that in the night.

The fifth and the sixth and seventh
Exclaim, 'It was fun to take part.'
For some, that is true, but the others
Are feeling dejected at heart.

Sing praise to the losers of racers
Who wave as tears spill from their eyes
For though they are given no medal
They will be the first to grow wise.

Going swimming

What will you wear to go swimming?
Something all jazzy and bright!
Something that fits like it's meant to –
neither too loose nor too tight.

What will you wear to go swimming?
Something that makes you look good!
Check carefully in the mirror
that it will hide what it should!

What will you wear to go swimming?
Something that feels all soft!
But take care: it feels like nothing
if, when you dive, it comes off.

The regulation swimming hat

No one can go in the pool without a swimming hat.
It's got to be the proper regulation one at that.
The trouble is that swimming hats can easily be lost
when in amongst the shoes and socks and towels
 they are tossed.
My mother said, 'I know the trick, I'll get a huge
 supply
and then we'll know we've always got another one
 that's dry.'
I think she bought a million once summer had
 begun.
And now, with three weeks left to go, we're down
 to only one.

All the kit

I have the snazziest swimsuit
I have the jazziest towel
I have the funkiest waterproof bag
that makes all my classmates go, 'Wow!'

I have the grooviest goggles
complete with a bit for my nose
but I can't go swimming at all this term 'cos
there's fungus between all my toes.

Sports day

We're getting in training for sports day
But no, we're not practising races
We spent half the lesson just cleaning our shoes
And rubbing the mud off our laces.

We're getting in training for sports day
Of course we don't jog round the track
We're practising taking the chairs to the field
And then taking all of them back.

We're getting in training for sports day
It should be the best one in years
We've never done star-jumps or press-ups
But – YAY! – have we practised our cheers!

39 Siblings

If you're an only child you might dream of having brothers and sisters. Those with brothers and sisters might dream of being an only child!

A school of your own

I don't think that brothers and sisters
should ever be in the same school,
'cos one of them's just that bit cleverer so
the other one feels a fool.

Not like my sister

You're so like your sister,
they all say to me.
Is that what a boy wants to hear?
Most certainly not,
and if you say the same
I'll give you a clip round the ear.

Wrong name

I answered the phone and this silly voice said,
'Can I speak to your sister Fran, please?'
I yelled up the stairs, 'Oi, Fran, it's for you,
it's a girl, and it sounds like Louise.'
So Fran grabbed the phone, first she giggled, then
    gasped,
then gave me a look that could kill.
The person who squeaked with a voice like a girl
was some twit that she fancies, named Will.

Family fights

If I irritate my sister
just like she irritates me
I think she might go off in a huff:
right where I want her to be.

And if I annoy my brother
and drive him right up the wall,
he'll think of a way to get back at me,
I don't fancy that at all.

Football in the family

Football with mates is the best way to play
while family can get a bit shirty,
but never, don't ever, play in a mixed team
'cos that is when football gets dirty.

40 Holidays

At last.

Down by the sea

The waves roll in from the glittering green
   of the sparkling summertime sea.
They curl and unfurl on the golden sand
   and run up the beach to me.

The waves roll out to the beautiful blue
   where the ocean touches the sky.
They swish and they slide with the silver tide
   and shyly they say goodbye.

The holiday flight

Lord, keep us safe this night
Secure from all our fears
May angels guard us while we sleep
Till morning light appears.

Lord, keep us safe this flight
And keep the aircraft whole
Please keep it working properly,
O Guardian of my soul.

Lord, keep us safe this flight
I do not understand
Just how the air can hold us as
We fly to other lands.

Lord, keep us safe this flight
Securely in our seat
No turbulence to trouble us
No luggage on our feet.

Lord, keep us safe this flight
Secure from every fear
May angels watch us in the sky
Till airport lights appear.

* First verse by John Leland (1754–1841)

I wanted to send you a postcard

I wanted to send you a postcard
But couldn't find one of the sky
On the day when the wind made my kite dip
   and dive
And set the clouds dancing on by.

I wanted to send you postcard
But couldn't find one of the wave
That I rode to the shore as the surf crashed
   and roared
And I felt oh so clever and brave.

I wanted to send you a postcard
But couldn't find words that would say
The feeling inside the adventures
I had on my holiday.

Never go off camping

Never go off camping
until you've checked your tent
and sorted all the bits that have gone missing
   or got bent.

Never go off camping
without a decent mat:
you're bound to end up pitching on some ground
   that isn't flat.

Never go off camping
unless your sleeping bag
is clean and warm and cosy
not some thin and lumpy rag.

Never go off camping
unless your torch is bright
and take extra batteries
for that dark and scary night.

Never go off camping
unless you've checked the weather:
you might just find that staying home
is better altogether.

Staying home

I'm not looking forward to summer
I don't want to have weeks off school
There's nothing exciting that's happening
In fact, nothing's happening at all.

I don't have a dad who's a pilot
We don't have a villa in Spain
I'm not going walking on Exmoor
I'm just staying home once again.

There's one dull adventure playground
And some stupid open-air pool
And weeks to hang out doing nothing.
On second thoughts, that could be cool.

Index of First Lines